Family Therapy Glossary

Edited by
Craig A. Everett

AMERICAN ASSOCIATION FOR
MARRIAGE AND FAMILY THERAPY
Washington, DC

Published by
American Association for Marriage and Family Therapy
1133 15th Street, NW, Suite 300
Washington, DC 20005-2710
(202) 452-0109

FAMILY THERAPY GLOSSARY (third edition) / Craig A. Everett, editor.
Copyright © 2000 by the American Association for Marriage and Family Therapy. All rights reserved. Printed in the United States of America. No part of this publication may be reproduced, stored in a retrieval system, or transmitted, in any form or by any means, electronic, mechanical, photocopying, recording, or otherwise, without the prior written permission of the publisher.

Library of Congress Catalog Card Number 00-134465

Editor
Craig A. Everett, Ph.D.

Contributing Editors
Lee Bowen, Ph.D.
Steve Livingston, Ph.D.
Marriage and Family Therapy Program
Department of Psychiatry and Behavioral Science
Mercer University
Macon, Georgia

Gregory W. Brock, Ph.D.
Marriage and Family Therapy Program
Department of Family Studies
University of Kentucky
Lexington, Kentucky

Jo Ellen Patterson, Ph.D.
Todd M. Edwards, Ph.D.
Marriage and Family Therapy Program
School of Education
University of San Diego
San Diego, California

Contributors

University of Kentucky
Betty Christine Gross
Leontyne Gulley
Eric Harms
Michael Hench
Brent Hutchinson
Sharletta Mahone
Nicholle Moore
Katie Neuman
Tiffaney Parkinson

University of San Diego
Karen Banks
Sara Bisono-Gonzalez
Denice Davis
Kimber Napierskie,
David Shoemaker
Nichole Smith
Maria Vazquez

Mercer University
Barbara Gaughf
Mary Key
Sylvia Stapleton
Gene Wells

Craig A. Everett, Ph.D., is Director of the Arizona Institute of Family Therapy and a family therapist in private practice in Tucson, Arizona. He is a Past President of the American Association for Marriage and Family Therapy, formerly director of AAMFT accredited graduate programs at Florida State University and Auburn University, and editor of the *Journal of Divorce and Remarriage*.

The Contributors to this edition were all master's students in the three respective programs.

The original *Family Therapy Glossary* was published in 1984. Co-editors of the 1984 edition were Vincent D. Foley, Ph.D., and Craig A. Everett, Ph.D. Contributing Editors were Lee Combrinck-Graham, Ph.D., Sandra L. Halperin, Ph.D., and William C. Nichols, Ed.D.

The Editor of the second edition in 1992 was Craig A. Everett, Ph.D. Contributing Editors were James Keller, Ph.D. and Candyce S. Russell, Ph.D.

The American Association for Marriage and Family Therapy (AAMFT) is the professional association for the field of marriage and family therapy; its membership is made up of marriage and family therapists from the United States, Canada, and abroad.

The purposes of AAMFT are to represent the professional interests of marriage and family therapists; facilitate research, theory development, and education in the field of marriage and family therapy; and develop standards for graduate education and training, clinical supervision, professional ethics, and the clinical practice of marriage and family therapy.

Introduction

The first edition of the *Family Therapy Glossary,* published by the American Association for Marriage and Family Therapy (AAMFT) in 1982, was intended to capture the "evolving" field of family therapy at the beginning of that decade. It was compiled at a time when most of the pioneers in family therapy were still teaching and writing. Many of the early terms included in that first edition had dual meanings because they were borrowed from usage in the broader fields of psychotherapy and mental health. Other terms were developed uniquely by these pioneers in their own early family therapy theories and clinical models.

The second edition of the *Glossary* (1992), which appeared early in the 1990s, was published to coincide with AAMFT's fiftieth anniversary in 1992. It marked the achievement of marriage and family therapy's emergence and recognition as a mental health provider among the other mental health disciplines. The literature and research of the MFT field at that time had evolved a formidable body of knowledge. The goal in the compilation of that edition was to identify concepts and terminology that were central to the field and yet maintain a balance with the continuing historical resources of the past.

The publication of this third edition marks the continuing growth and contributions of AAMFT and the MFT field in the new millenium. The goal continues to be to identify concepts and terms which reflect both the core and the growing edge of the MFT field. The challenge is greater to maintain the balance with the historical resources as we are another decade removed from the contributions of the field's pioneers. The volume of new concepts and terms to be added to this edition were much less, as compared to the process in 1982 and 1992. Therefore, an additional focus here was to update and revise continuing concepts to reflect their present usage and to retain historical terms that are either still used widely or, in a few cases, that retain a certain colorful contribution to the field.

The first edition of the *Glossary* became a resource for practitioners, educators, and clinical graduate students across the mental health disciplines. It was used in popular literature and public programs, and became AAMFT's best seller. The goal of this edition remains the same, and is consistent with the early goal stated by William C. Nichols in the foreword to the first edition of the *Glossary:*

Family Therapy Glossary

"...To go beyond the level of provincialism and personalities and to set forth a glossary of terms that had achieved general standing and acceptance in the family therapy field."

MFT graduate students from three master's programs in marriage and family therapy, all affiliated with AAMFT, were enlisted to ensure that the final product reflected accurately the cutting edge of the field. (The development of the second edition similarly used MFT graduate students.) MFT faculty from each of the three graduate programs served as Contributing Editors and coordinated the review and critique of present terms and the introduction of new terms.

The definitions are not intended to be comprehensive but to convey a recognition of central concepts, terms, and clinical models. Each is cross-referenced internally so that the reader can follow both theoretical threads as well as other supporting concepts that appear throughout the *Glossary*. Specific terms that occur within definitions and that have been defined elsewhere in the *Glossary* appear in italics. Parenthetical notes at the end of many of the definitions refer the reader to other supporting concepts throughout the *Glossary*. The references are not intended to be exhaustive but to identify, in most cases, either the earliest definition of the term or the major published work in which the term was introduced or explicated. Some of the definitions contain both early references and contemporary references.

As the third edition of the *Glossary* appears at the beginning of the millenium, the family therapy field has continued to gain ground and influence, not only among the other mental health disciplines, but in the eyes of the public as well. The field's body of knowledge, based on both theory and research, is more established. It is the hope of the editors and AAMFT that this edition of the *Family Therapy Glossary* will continue to be a timely and useful resource for the present and evolving generation of family therapists.

Craig A. Everett, Ph.D.
Tucson, Arizona

TERMS AND DEFINITIONS

ACCOMMODATION

A process from *Structural Family Therapy* by which a family therapist adjusts and modifies one's role during a clinical session to feedback received from the family system in order to achieve *joining*. (Aponte & VanDeusen, 1991; Minuchin, 1974) [See *joining, Structural Family Therapy*]

ALLIANCE

A concept from family systems theory that identifies the affiliations between two or more family members, based on common interests or shared beliefs, but without the intent to keep others out (as in a *coalition*); or, simply, an attraction by certain members within a subgroup. (Hoffman, 1981; Wynne, 1961) [See *coalition*]

AESTHETICS

As the complement of *pragmatics,* this term refers to a sensitivity toward holism, complexity, and the larger patterns which connect family members. An aesthetic family therapist views therapy as an art and focuses more on patterns and holism and less on techniques. It has been asserted that to be successful, therapists must work from both an aesthetic and pragmatic position (Keeney, 1983; Keeney & Sprenkle, 1982) [See *pragmatics*]

ALTERNATIVE STORY

A concept from *Narrative Family Therapy* which defines the meaning ascribed to a "lived experience" by a family member that contradicts or falls outside of the member's or family's *dominant narrative.* (White & Epston, 1990) [See *dominant narrative, Narrative Family Therapy*]

ANALOGIC

A form of communication, defined in systems theory, which consists of quantities, differences and analogies. Analogic communication has connotative (as opposed to denotative) meaning. Such communication consists not of words, but of the nonverbal, paraverbal, and contextual aspects of interaction. Family therapists refer to analogic communication when they identify the process (as opposed to the content) of a family therapy session. (Bateson, 1972, 1979; Watzlawick, Beavin & Jackson, 1967) [See *digital*]

BATTLE FOR INITIATIVE

A clinical goal, developed in *Symbolic-experiential Family Therapy*, to get the family to take responsibility for what happens in the therapy process. Napier and Whitaker (1978) believed that the family therapist must allow the family to take responsibility for change in therapy by shifting the responsibility for agenda-making and the initiation of change to the family. (Whitaker & Bumberry, 1988; Napier & Whitaker, 1978) [See *battle for structure, Symbolic-experiential Family Therapy*]

BATTLE FOR STRUCTURE

A clinical goal, developed in *Symbolic-experiential Family Therapy*, to establish the necessary ground rules or structure for therapy with a family. For example, these would include the concerns of which members should attend the first session and how the therapy process should proceed. Napier and Whitaker (1978) believed that the therapist must "win" this battle in order to establish a trustworthy therapeutic relationship. (Weber & Levine, 1995; Whitaker & Bumberry, 1988; Napier & Whitaker, 1978) [See *battle for initiative, Symbolic-experiential Family Therapy*]

BEHAVIORAL FAMILY THERAPY

A clinical model which utilizes learning theory and is often integrated with resources from cognitive therapy. It begins with a problem analysis to: 1) pinpoint specific behaviors that are causing distress; 2) prioritize the range of problems; and 3) determine the frequency of the problem behavior. The family therapist then redefines the problems at a family systems level to define the antecedents and consequences. The goal is to define the problem in overt behavioral terms and then to develop achievable goals with problem-solving solutions in which all family members can participate. These interventions may include education, communication training, and contingency contracting.

(Weeks & Treat, 1992; Falloon, 1991; Jacobson & Holtzworth-Munroe, 1986; Holtzworth-Munroe, 1991; Jacobson & Margolin, 1979; Patterson, Reid, Jones, & Conger, 1975)

BORDERLINE PROCESS

A clinical process which describes a cluster of symptoms associated with the Borderline Personality Disorder, but which occur, not just in a diagnosed individual, but are present and identifiable throughout several generations of a family system. The patterns which appear in a family system include *splitting* and reciprocal *projective identification* among family members, typically children in coexisting triangles, such that one child is perceived as good (*good object*) and another as bad (*bad object*). (Everett & Everett, 1997; Everett, Halperin, Volgy, & Wissler, 1989) [See *good/bad objects, projective identification, splitting*]

BOUNDARIES

A concept [See Figure 1], developed in *Structural Family Therapy,* which identifies abstract dividers that are present between family *subsystems.* They may be defined spatially by the way family

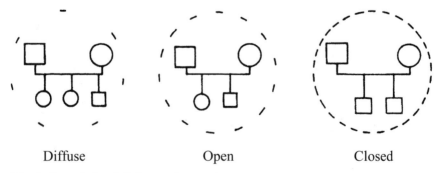

Diffuse　　　　　　　Open　　　　　　　Closed

Fig. 1. Boundaries defining nuclear systems

members align structurally with one another. Boundaries are set by the implicit rules defining who participates, and how, within each subsystem. They may be altered over time as the nature of the subsystems and the family's environment changes. Family therapists often describe them as rigid, flexible, diffuse, *open*, or *closed*. (Minuchin, 1974) [See *closed systems, open systems, Structural Family Therapy, subsystems*]

BRIEF FAMILY THERAPY

A clinical model directed toward brief problem resolution with the goal of helping family members change their responses to specific problems. It is based on two central notions: 1) that the family member's complaint is the actual problem and not a symptom of other underlying or historical issues; and 2) prior solutions attempted by the family have served only to reinforce the problematic behavior. This is a time-limited, pragmatic, nonhistorical, step-by-step *strategic* approach based on an understanding of family behavior which suggests that most problems result from the mishandling of normal life difficulties. The therapist's role is to discover what keeps the problematic behavior persisting and what is needed to change it. (Nichols & Schwartz, 1998; Segal, 1991; DeShazer, 1988, 1985, 1982; Fisch, Weakland, & Segal, 1982; Watzlawick, Weakland & Fisch, 1974) [See *Solution-focused Family Therapy, Strategic Family Therapy*]

CENTRIPETAL FAMILY PATTERN

This clinical pattern [See Figure 2] which describes a process of "binding" family members tightly and rigidly within an isolating family system. For example, at adolescent separation, children may view themselves as too weak to leave the family and they are, in fact, rewarded by parents for remaining at home. (Stierlin, 1974) [See *centrifugal family pattern*]

CENTRIFUGAL FAMILY PATTERN

This clinical pattern [See Figure 2] which describes a process of "expelling" family members early and forcefully from the family system, particularly at the stage of adolescent separation. These family systems often lack internal at-

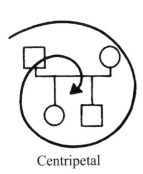
Centripetal

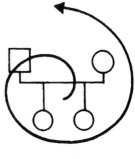
Centrifugal

Fig. 2. Centripetal and centrifugal family patterns

tachment and cohesiveness, and the adolescent is compelled to try to find with one's peers the closeness she/he has failed to experience within their family. (Stierlin, 1974) [See *centripetal family pattern*]

CIRCULAR CAUSALITY

A concept from systems theory which refers to the non-linear, recursive nature of the interaction in family systems, as well as in other organized systems, where the behavior of one component effects the behavior of a second component which effects the behavior of a third which, reciprocally, effects the behavior of the first component. This process implies that behavior may be based as much on the interactional dynamics of a system as on the internal psychological processes of each member. It also defines the interconnectedness of family experiences and suggests that causality within a system may be basically circular rather than *linear*. (Nichols & Schwartz, 1998; Wynne, 1988; Dell, 1985; Hoffman, 1981; Bateson, 1972) [See *epistemology, epistemological error, linear causality*]

CIRCULAR QUESTIONING

A clinical technique, developed by the Milan group of family therapists, which describes a goal of eliciting differences in perceptions about events, problems, and/or relationships from each family member. It is based on the premise that family members frequently describe a problem in terms that are often too broad or too narrow. It suggests two types of questions: 1) ones that identify connections and broaden a member's understanding of their larger context; and 2) ones that draw distinctions and narrow a member's focus from generalizations. (Nichols & Schwartz, 1998; Brown, 1997; Tomm, 1987, 1988; Palazolli, Boscolo, Cecchin, & Prata, 1978)

CLOSED SYSTEMS

A concept which describes family systems which are self-contained and often isolated by their limited recognition and use of feedback, as compared to *open systems* which utilize free exchange of information with their external environment to alter internal interactions. A closed family system is often organized to preserve its status quo and to resist change. (Von Bertalanffy, 1974, 1968) [See *boundaries, open systems*]

COACH

A role of a family therapist, developed initially by Murray Bowen, where one functions both as a role model for individual family members in their *differentiation* process and as a facilitator of *family of origin* exploration. The therapist encourages the family members to work on solving their own problems rather than functioning in the role of an "expert." This role is also present in the *Symbolic-experiential* model. (Becvar & Becvar, 1996; Kerr & Bowen, 1988; Bowen, 1978) [See *differentiation of self, family of origin, Family of Origin Family Therapy, Symbolic-Experiential Therapy*]

COALITION

A family dynamic which occurs when two members join together, often covertly, against a third member; sometimes referred to as a relational *triangle*. Coalitions in family systems may cross generational *boundaries,* such as when a child and one parent form a coalition against the other parent, or when a grandparent and child form a coalition against a parent. Haley (1963) asserted that the forming and reforming of coalitions may serve to keep the power distribution in a system more nearly balanced. (Haley, 1963) [See *boundaries, triangles*]

The term may also refer to an "unbalancing" clinical technique in which the therapist joins with one member of the family system, or with one *subsystem*, in order to imbalance a part of the system and re-establish more appropriate subsystem boundaries and decrease distance between members of that system or subsystem. (Minuchin & Fishman, 1981; Minuchin, 1974) [See *Structural Family Therapy*]

COGNITIVE FAMILY THERAPY

A clinical model, developed initially by Albert Ellis and Aaron Beck, and often integrated with *Behavioral Family Therapy,* which is based on the assumption that behavior and affect follow from thinking. In family systems each family member's beliefs about one another will affect their patterns of interaction. For example, if a spouse returns home with a depressive and agitated mood, the partner may assume (incorrectly) that she/he is the cause of the spouse's mood and withdraw. The goal is to restructure and redefine such distorted beliefs to change the dysfunctional behavioral patterns. (Nichols & Schwartz, 1998; Epstein & Schlesinger, 1996; Weeks & Treat, 1992) [See *Behavioral Family Therapy*]

COHERENCE

A process in family systems whereby the various components of a family fit together. The coherence unique to a particular system determines the ways in which that family behaves and interacts. (Dell, 1982)

COHESION

A concept from family systems theory that defines the emotional bonding among family members. According to the Circumplex Model of family systems (Olson, 1993), family cohesion may be measured along a continuum ranging from "disengaged" (very low cohesion) to "separated" (low to moderate cohesion) to "connected" (moderate to high cohesion) to "enmeshed" (very high cohesion). The central categories of "separated" and "connected" are thought to lead to optimal family functioning. (Olson, 1993)

COLLABORATION

A process central to the practice of *Medical Family Therapy* in which health care providers, including family therapists, physicians, nurse practitioners, and psychiatrists, work together in the care of patients. The goal is an integrative paradigm for thinking about health and mental health problems, and treatment. (Seaburn, Lorenz, Gunn, Gawinski, & Mauksch, 1996; McDaniel, Hepworth, & Doherty, 1992) [See *ecosystemic perspective, Medical Family Therapy*]

COLLABORATIVE LANGUAGE SYSTEMS

A clinical concept, developed in relation to *postmodern* thought and social constructionism, which emphasizes a nonhierarchical partnership between the family therapist and the family system.

It focuses on the meaning that family members' attach to their experiences and the language that they use to construct their meanings. The goal is a respectful, generative conversation in which individuals learn to talk "with" rather than "to" one another. (Anderson, 1995; Anderson & Goolishian, 1992) [See *constructivism, postmodernism*]

COLLABORATIVE THERAPY

A forerunner to the *conjoint* method in which separate therapists treated different family members (usually spouses) individually. For example, in the early child guidance movement where the child, as the identified patient, would have been interviewed by a child psychiatrist while the parents were interviewed by a social worker. In marital therapy each spouse would have been treated by different but "collaborating" therapists. (Martin, 1976) [See *concurrent therapy, conjoint therapy*]

COLLUSION

A process in family systems where members attribute to one another shared feelings which serve to support certain beliefs or protective functions of the system. For example, family members may maintain certain rigid and stereotypical roles that may appear to outside observers as dysfunctional. However, within the family system, these roles or beliefs may function to protect, stabilize, and balance the system's ongoing interactions. Spouses in a marital relationship may collude to protect one another's innermost secrets and thus maintain the status quo of the relationship. (Boszormenyi-Nagy & Krasner, 1986; Dicks, 1967) [See *quid pro quo*]

COMMUNICATION

A central concept in family systems theory whereby members share meaning with each other, both verbally and non-verbally. Certain types of communication are defined as *digital,* which define the content of what is expressed, or *analogic,* which identifies how the content is processed and how it defines the relationship between members. For example, nonverbal behavior may "cancel out" a verbal message such as when the verbal expression of affection occurs with abuse.

An early model of family therapy based on communication issues, developed by Virginia Satir, suggested that communication which is clear, direct, and person-centered, and in which the verbal and non-verbal messages are congruent, would be considered healthy and growth-enhancing. In contrast, communications which contain many "mixed messages" may contribute to family conflict and dysfunctions (Satir, 1967). [See *conjoint family therapy*]

Behavioral approaches to family therapy often emphasize training in communication skills to help family members develop more positive interaction as a foundation for cooperative problem solving. (Faloon, 1991; Jacobson & Margolin, 1979) [See *Behavioral Family Therapy*]

COMPLEMENTARITY

An early concept in family theory and utilized in marital therapy which describes the manner in which each partner complements, fulfills, or is expected to fulfill, the unconscious needs and role expectations of the other partner—a mutual "fitting together" in a relationship. Complementary marital patterns include: nurturance–dependence, gregarious–private, and spontaneous–controlling. The complementarity dynamic maintains the equilibrium of the dyadic system but also may reinforce dysfunctional elements. (Walters, Carter, Papp, & Silverstein, 1988; Beavers, 1977; Skynner, 1976; Dicks, 1967; Winch, 1954)

At an interactional systems level, the behaviors and/or emotionality of one partner may be enhanced by corresponding behaviors and emotions of the other. For example, one spouse may be assertive and the other submissive such that these characteristic behaviors complement one another and support the relationship. (Watzlawick, Beavin, & Jackson, 1967) [See *symmetrical*]

CONCURRENT THERAPY

An early treatment method whereby marital therapists attempted to preserve traditional concerns of *confidentiality* and *transference* by treating each spouse separately in individual sessions rather then *conjointly*. (Martin, 1976) [See *collaborative therapy, conjoint therapy*]

CONFIDENTIALITY

A professional concept that refers to the ethical obligation of a therapist to protect client information, identity, and privacy. For family therapists, this obligation is more complex due to working with multiple family members. It also involves privacy issues among and between family members, as well as external sources. The process of revealing information to parties, either within or outside of the family system, as well as the therapist's responsibilities and conditions under which confidentiality may be waived, are outlined by state laws and the *Code of Ethics* of the American Association for Marriage and Family Therapy (1999).

CONFLICT INDUCTION

A clinical technique from *Structural Family Therapy* whereby a family's conflict-avoiding mechanisms are blocked by the family therapist and conflict-arousing issues are introduced to the system, such that the family must develop new ways of managing and resolving conflicts. (Minuchin, 1974) [See *Structural Family Therapy*]

CONJOINT FAMILY THERAPY

This historically defined clinical model, perhaps the earliest definition of family systems therapy, broke the traditions of psychotherapy when it advocated that a single therapist could effectively treat a marriage by seeing *both spouses together in the same session*. This was in contrast to the accepted *concurrent* and *collaborative* methods. It was a radical departure from traditional psychoanalytic methods of working only with individuals around *transference* phenomena. Today this term refers more broadly to most family systems interventions that involve working with multiple family members together. (Satir, 1967) [See *collaborative therapy, concurrent therapy, transference*]

CONSTITUTIONALIST PERSPECTIVE

A concept from *Narrative Family Therapy* in which the meaning ascribed to one's "lived experiences" is authored (constituted) through dominant narratives and alternative stories. This model assumes that an individual's understanding of their past, present, and future is constructed and shaped by the meaning attached to their lived experiences. (White, 1992) [See *Narrative Family Therapy*]

CONSTRUCTIVISM

A concept from systems theory and *epistemology* which asserts that reality is created through the process of interacting with one's environment rather than by discovery, that reality is constructed in one's mind through perturbations from the environment. In contrast, the traditional scientific method asserts that an objective reality is an actuality independent of one's existence, and social constructionism views the construction of reality emerging from social interchange and mediated through language. (Hoffman, 1992; White & Epston, 1990; Held, 1990; Efran, Lukens, & Lukens, 1988) [See *epistemology*]

CONTEXTUAL FAMILY THERAPY

A clinical model, developed by Ivan Boszormenyi-Nagy, which suggests that family behavior is strongly influenced by "invisible," *intergenerational loyalties,* or bonds across generations, which involve transgenerational *entitlements,* and indebtedness. It identifies a broad range of relational determinants: individual and transactional systems, transgenerational patterns, and relational ethics. The goal of the family therapist is to assist families in exploring their legacies and determining how they can go about "balancing the ledger of obligation" to past, present, and future generations. (Boszormenyi-Nagy & Krasner, 1986; Boszormenyi-Nagy & Spark, 1973) [See *entitlement, intergenerational accounting, intergenerational loyalties*]

COUNTERPARADOX

A clinical concept, originated by the Milan family therapy group, which refers to changing the paradoxical nature of a family in which symptomatic behavior actually maintains the *homeostatic* and often dysfunctional tendencies in a system. For example, in response to a system's resistance to change, the therapy team may offer a *counterparadoxical* message prescribing "no change" based upon *positive connotation,* interpreting all family behavior as good, which preserves the cohesion of the group. (Campbell, Draper, & Crutchley, 1991; Tomm, 1984; Palazolli, Boscolo, Cecchin, & Prata, 1978) [See *counterparadox, homeostatic, positive connotation*]

COUNTERTRANSFERENCE

A concept in psychotherapy which defines personal or "distorted" feelings which may develop in the therapist toward their client. In family therapy, this term refers to distortion engendered in the therapist in response to a certain aspect of the clinical family system's structure or behaviors. The therapist may re-experience aspects of her/his own family of origin experiences which may be triggered by the family in treatment. While these responses may be difficult to bring to awareness, they may become clinical data that will be useful in the treatment process with the family. For example, a therapist who understands his or her own fearful response to a client may use that information to better understand the feelings elicited from the family members by the client. (Whitaker, 1982) [See *transference*]

CULTURAL SENSITIVITY

A clinical concern which refers to the integration of cultural perspectives in the work of family therapists. According to Falicov (1988), this integration is accomplished through two processes: 1) developing an ecosystemic view that constantly places the family in its social context, and 2) focusing on the degree of cultural consonance-dissonance between the world view of the family and that of the therapist. (Falicov, 1988)

CYBERNETICS

An area of study from systems theory, originally defined by Norbert Weiner as the science of communication and control, which entered the family therapy field through the work of Bateson, Jackson, Haley, and Weakland. Bateson (1972, 1979) suggested, epistemologically, that one lives in an ecosystemic world which functions like a gigantic mind. Others have operationalized this concept clinically by suggesting that the descriptions of a family system and interventions toward a system cannot be separated from the distinctions which are drawn by the observer who is describing and working with that system. (Watzlawick, 1984; Keeney, 1983; Greenberg, 1977; Bateson, 1972, 1979) [See *epistemology*]

DECONSTRUCTION

A term from *Narrative Family Therapy* which describes a procedure to "subvert" the "taken for granted" realities that often "oppress" family members. It is used clinically to "take apart the problem saturated story" of a family system. This lead to "externalizing" conversations about the problem and "re-authoring" its meaning. (White 1997, 1992) [See *constitutionalist perspective, Narrative Family Therapy*]

DEFINITIONAL CEREMONY

A clinical intervention from *Narrative Family Therapy* which involves three stages: 1) "tellings," 2) "retellings of the telling," and 3) "retellings of the retellings." The individual or family begins the process by telling their story in front of an audience. The audience, or "outsider witness group" then retells the story with an emphasis on a particular quality or skill of the ones who told the story. Finally, the original story tellers reflect on what they have heard in the retelling. (White, 1997) [See *Narrative Family Therapy*]

DELEGATION

A process in family systems whereby a family member, often a child, is prescribed a particular role or mission, usually directed by the parents or from intergenerational sources, and subsequently acts out aspects of this role within the family or the community. The purpose of the role may be to diffuse conflict in other areas of the family and may serve to rebalance the dysfunctional patterns of the system. (Stierlin, 1974) [See *parentification, scapegoating*]

DETRIANGULATION

A clinical technique, developed by Murray Bowen, which involves the gradual separation of one or more family members from a dysfunctional *triangular* relationship. (Kerr & Bowen, 1988; Bowen, 1978) [See *Family of Origin Therapy, triangles*]

DEVIATION AMPLIFICATION

An early cybernetic term which described the process in a system where uncorrected positive feedback produced an escalation of symptoms. For example, high conflict in a dyadic relationship may escalate into abusive behaviors toward one another. (Hoffman, 1973) [See *runaway*]

DIFFERENTIATION OF SELF

A concept from *Family of Origin Therapy* which defines a family member's ability to function autonomously in the context of being emotionally connected to other members. It has also been used to describe the process whereby a family member learns to regulate anxiety by objectively coordinating thinking with emotional responses. (Jones, 1994; Schnarch, 1991; Kerr & Bowen, 1988; Bowen, 1978) [See *Family of Origin Therapy*]

DIGITAL

A concept that describes a form of communication which utilizes arbitrary signs which "stand for" something in a one-to-one relationship. For example, the word "bed" stands for the piece of furniture on which one sleeps. Family therapists utilize this concept when they identify the content (as opposed to the process—*analogic*) of a family therapy session. (Bateson, 1972, 1979; Watzlawick, Beavin & Jackson, 1967) [See *analogic*]

DISENGAGING FAMILY SYSTEMS

A pattern or typology which identifies a family system where there are present strong and impenetrable internal *boundaries* (i.e., between individuals and/or subsystems) while there may be more diffuse external boundaries around the system. These systems often promote separation at the expense of family belonging and may fail to provide intimacy and support for individual family members. Family members may separate and leave this type of system readily because there are fewer emotional bonds and loyalties. (Minuchin, 1974) [See *boundaries, centrifugal family pattern, enmeshing family systems*]

DIVORCE MEDIATION

A clinical model, which may be performed by a trained therapist, attorney, or conflict resolution specialist, that offers divorcing families an alternative to the traditional legal adversarial process. The goal is to help divorcing spouses in work out a self-determined divorce agreement which may include a settlement of issues such as child custody and access, child support, spousal maintenance, and the division of debts and assets. It has been shown to be more cost effective to the family than traditional divorce litigation. (Erickson & McKnight, 2000; Erickson & Erickson, 1998; Hughes & Kirby, 2000; Everett & Everett, 1994; Marlow & Sauber, 1990; Folberg & Milne, 1988; Everett, 1985, Haynes, 1981) [See *divorce therapy*]

DIVORCE THERAPY

A stage of intervention or clinical services, rather than a formal model or technique, with the goal of working with divorcing families to assist them in dealing with concerns such as detaching from the relationship, understanding their ambivalence, planning a physical separation for them and their children, defining the ongoing needs of the children, and planning their subsequent parenting roles. Following the dissolution, the family therapist focuses on such issues as postdivorce adjustment, re-establishing a social network, managing relations with the former spouse, co-parenting roles, and potentially re-marriage. (Kaslow, 1995, 1981; Everett & Volgy, 1991; Crosby, 1989; Sprenkle & Storm, 1983) [See *divorce mediation*]

DOMINANT NARRATIVE

A concept from *Narrative Family Therapy* which identifies the beliefs, values, practices, and normative standards of a society's dominant culture. These narratives represent prevailing social constructions of the individuals within the dominant culture and not "objective realities." (Freedman & Combs, 1996; White & Epston, 1990) [See *alternative story, Narrative Family Therapy*]

DOUBLE-BIND   BATESON

An early concept in family systems which defined a process whereby a specific message was stated but also contradicted simultaneously by a second mutually exclusive message. This occurred in the context of a close relationship where the recipient of these messages was confused and unable to comment on *(metacommunicate)* the perceived contradiction. It was once hypothesized, but later discounted, that this phenomena could form the etiology of schizophrenia. (Watzlawick, Beavin, & Jackson, 1967; Bateson, Jackson, Haley & Weakland, 1956) [See *metacommunication*]

ECOSYSTEMIC APPROACH

A theoretical model which encourages family therapists to identify broader systems that influence the family: e.g., gender, culture, religion, health systems, neighborhoods. Goals of this model involve biopsychosocial interventions between systems and *collaboration* between the family and social resources. (Seaburn, Landau-Stanton, & Horwitz, 1995; Keeney, 1983; Keeney & Sprenkle, 1982; Aponte, 1980; Epstein, Bishop, & Levin, 1978; Auerswald, 1968) [See *collaboration, Medical Family Therapy*]

ELICITATION APPROACH

A clinical intervention used in marital therapy in which a couple's sexual behaviors (including the style and content included, and excluded in their repertoire) become a window from which the therapist can understand the partners' individual and relational functioning. (Schnarch, 1991)

EMOTIONAL CUTOFF

A concept, developed by Murray Bowen, which identifies a pattern of dramatic emotional (and often geographical) separation between an individual and one's family of origin. This pattern often leads to a process of *fusion* with other individuals, such as spouses or children, who replace the ties to the family of origin system. (Kerr & Bowen, 1988; Bowen, 1978) [See *Family of Origin Therapy, fusion*]

ENACTMENT

A clinical technique, developed in *Structural Family Therapy*, whereby the therapist encourages the family to demonstrate in action a behavioral sequence that replicates their normal interactions or encourages the practice of a new type of interaction. For example, the therapist may have a meal with the family of an anorexic adolescent, or ask them to simulate such an activity, which allows the family to enact for the therapist their specific behaviors which involve eating. (Minuchin, 1974) [See *Structural Family Therapy*]

ENMESHING FAMILY SYSTEMS

A pattern or typology which identifies a family system of diffuse internal *boundaries* (i.e., between individuals and subsystems) and often closed external boundaries. These systems display a high degree of emotional resonance and reactivity between members who may be over-concerned and over-involved in each other's lives. Such systems may delay separation and individuation of its members. (Minuchin, 1974) [See *boundaries, centripetal family pattern, disengaging family systems*]

ENTITLEMENT

A concept, defined by Boszormenyi-Nagy, which identifies a relational "credit" that family members may accumulate as a result of consideration offered to a parent or partner. It is seen in the balancing of parent–child relationships and can accumulate across generations. (Boszormenyi-Nagy & Spark, 1973) [See *Contextual Family Therapy, intergenerational loyalties*]

ENTROPY

A concept from systems theory which defines the theoretical tendency of matter to move toward randomness or an undifferentiated state, which can lead to disorder and loss of distinctive form. (Bateson, 1972) [See *negentropy*]

EPISTEMOLOGY

An area of philosophical thinking which describes the investigation of the origin and nature of knowledge, and how human beings know what they know. In family therapy, understanding the world view of a family's system helps to explain their behavior, as well as their symptoms. An epistemological perspective allows the therapist to *reframe* interventions that may alter the family's definition of reality (Keeney & Sprenkle, 1982; Maturana, 1978; Bateson, 1972)

EPISTEMOLOGICAL ERROR

A term used by Bateson to refer to any thinking or action which fails to recognize the circular nature of living systems. (Dell, 1985, 1982; Bateson, 1972) [See *circular causality, cybernetics, epistemology, linear causality*]

EQUIFINALITY

A concept from systems theory which suggests that similar outcomes may result from different origins, in contrast to the traditional cause-and-effect explanation. (Von Bertalanffy, 1974, 1968) [See *circular causality, equipotentiality, linear causality*]

EQUIPOTENTIALITY

A concept from systems theory which

defines the multiple possibilities of any event. As *equifinality* describes the possibility of similar outcomes resulting from different origins, this concept describes the principle that similar origins may result in different outcomes. Together these concepts express the notion that there are no single causes and effects. (Von Bertalanffy, 1974) [See *circular causality, equifinality, linear causality*]

ETHNICITY

A concept that refers to the unique social and historical heritage of a group of persons and to their values, shared meanings and goals. In family systems it describes the commonality of these issues which are transmitted within families over generations and may be reinforced by the surrounding community. Beyond race, religion, national and geographic origin, ethnicity involves conscious and unconscious processes that fulfill psychological needs for identity and historical continuity. It unites those who conceive of themselves as alike by virtue of their common ancestry, real or fictitious. Family therapists work to appreciate the ethnic heritage of client families as they find ways to join with them and assess resources that can be used in therapy. (Ariel, 1999; McGoldrick, Preto, Hines, & Lee, 1991; McGoldrick, Pearce, & Giordano, 1982)

EXCEPTION TO THE PROBLEM

A technique from *Solution Focused Family Therapy* which directs family members to search past and present experiences when the presenting problem did not exist, and thereby discover previously ignored solutions or understand differing contexts. (Berg & DeShazer, 1993; O'Hanlon & Weiner-Davis, 1989) [See *Solution Focused Family Therapy*]

EXONERATION

A process described in *Contextual Family Therapy* where adult children, through understanding intergenerational family dynamics and the potential victimization that may have occurred from one generation to the next, learn to forgive one's parents for past negative interactions. (Boszormenyi-Nagy & Spark, 1973) [See *Contextual Family Therapy, intergenerational loyalties*]

EXTERNALIZATION OF THE PROBLEM

A technique from *Narrative Family Therapy* that encourages family members to view problems as separate from themselves and "oppressive" such that the member's relationship to the problem becomes the clinical problem. A name may be assigned to the "problem story" and to the outcome ("counter plot"). (Freedman & Combs, 1996; White & Epston, 1990) [See *Narrative Family Therapy*]

FAMILY LIFE CYCLE

A concept from family theory which describes predictable patterns or cycles as a family progresses through developmental stages. Such stages may include: separation from family of origin, marriage, child bearing, child rearing, divorce, retirement, aging, and death. The family therapist attempts to normalize the family's presenting problem in the context of the family's respective developmental stage. (Carter & McGoldrick, 1989; Nichols, 1984)

FAMILY MAP

A concept (See Figure 3) from *Structural Family Therapy* which describes a visual and/or symbolic representation of a family system's organization and structure. It differs from a *genogram* by creating an arrangement of the family members around the presenting problem, and may illustrate the system's *coalitions* and *boundaries*. (Minuchin, 1974) [See *boundaries, coalitions, genograms, Structural Family Therapy*]

FAMILY MYTHS

A concept in family systems which describes stereotyped patterns of relating and functioning that are usually accepted and adhered to by all of the family members. Ferreira described this as "...A living and animated album of family pictures that no one quite dares to erase or throw away (1953, p. 460)." The myth is a broad illusion, commonly shared by family members, with a characteristic theme and internal rules, and serves to maintain the system's cohesiveness and stability. (Anderson & Bagarozzi, 1989; Ferreira, 1953)

FAMILY OF ORIGIN

A concept which defines the family origins of one's birth (i.e., biological family). The role that a family member plays within their family of procreation may be determined by her/his former roles in that family of origin. (Framo, 1992; Bowen, 1978) [See *Family of Origin Therapy*]

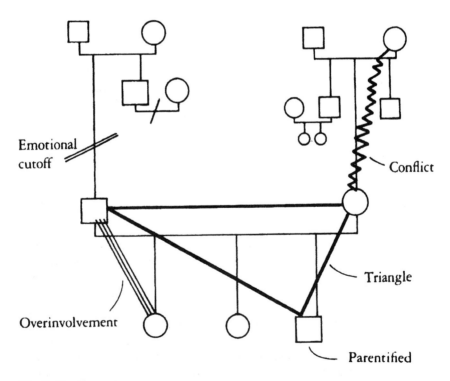

Fig. 3. Family map

FAMILY OF ORIGIN THERAPY

A clinical model, developed by Murray Bowen, which asserts that individuals and families should be understood in the context of their multiple generations and not as isolated individuals. Bowen believed that relationship patterns within the family system developed and repeated across the generations. He described eight interlocking concepts: *differentiation of self*, *triangles*, sibling position, nuclear family emotional processes, family projection process, *emotional cutoff*, multigenerational transmission, and societal emotional process. The goals include: 1) reducing the level of chronic anxiety in the family system; and 2) increasing the level of differentiation of self in family members in order to interrupt maladaptive relationship patterns (Framo, 1992; Kerr & Bowen, 1988; Bowen, 1978) [See *differentiation of self, emotional cutoff, multigenerational transmission process, triangles*]

FAMILY PROJECTION PROCESS

A concept, developed by Murray Bowen, which describes a process by which the levels of personal *differentiation* of the parents are passed on to their children. In other words, the levels of emotional functioning of the parents determine the levels of differentiation of the children. The concept explains how a given child may become the symptom bearer for the family. (Bowen, 1978) [See *differentiation of self, Family of Origin Therapy*]

The concept may also apply to the projection by the family of roles, values and other attributes onto spouses or children. [See *borderline process, good/bad objects, object relations, splitting*]

FAMILY RECONSTRUCTION

A clinical approach, developed by Virginia Satir, whereby family members are guided by the therapist back through stages of their lives in order to discover and unlock dysfunctional patterns from their past. (Satir, 1967)

FAMILY RITUALS

A concept in family systems which describes overt and/or covert patterns of actions and behaviors that are invoked to denote shared traditions, events, and celebrations. Family therapists may develop or prescribe alternative rituals to provide a family with structured interactions which offer new patterns of behavior or that will replace dysfunctional interactions. These prescribed rituals may also be planned to provide healing around such events as divorce, reconciliation, a young adult leaving home, or geographical relocation. (Imber-Black, 1988; Imber-Black, Roberts, & Whiting, 1988; Palazzoli, Boscolo, Cecchin, & Prata, 1978)

FAMILY RULES

A family systems concept that describes shared norms and values which govern general patterns of family functioning. Jackson (1965) differentiated "descriptive rules" as metaphors of regular interactive patterns and "prescriptive rules" as requirements for expected behavior. For example, in one family a rule may be that "disagreements are dangerous and may escalate into conflict and threats of violence." Family rules may be spoken or simply understood and internalized by family members. (Jackson, 1965)

FAMILY SECRETS

A concept from family systems which describes certain beliefs and attitudes, real or fantasized, which may be held privately by one family member, shared by others, or collusively subscribed to by all family members and passed from one generation to the next. Pincus and Dare (1978) suggested that secrets were based on power and dependence, love and hate "... feelings which are inevitably bound up with sex, birth, and death (p.16)." For example, parents may collusively keep the secret that their child was conceived "out of wedlock" and the child, and even her/his siblings, may carry the fantasy of being "adopted" based on random comments by extended family members. (Pincus & Dare, 1978) [See *family myths*]

FEEDBACK LOOPS

A concept from *cybernetic* theory which describes the process whereby the influence of any event comes back to itself through the other parts or events, and one point in a chain of events can reinitiate the entire chain of events. This concept helps family therapists understand the influence of multiple parts and events within a family system. (Hoffman, 1981; Bateson, 1972) [See *circular process, cybernetics*]

FEMINIST FAMILY THERAPY

A model intended to assist the family therapist in recognizing the impact of differing *gender role* socialization for men and women, of the differences in each gender's access to economic and social resources, and the primary role that women have been socialized to perform in family relations and child rearing. (Walters, Carter, Papp, & Silverstein, 1988) [See *gender roles, gender sensitivity*]

FIRST-ORDER CHANGE

A concept from systems theory that describes the process whereby changes in a system may leave unaltered the underlying (and potentially dysfunctional) organization of that system. For family therapists, a clinical family may be said to undergo first order change when it adapts or accommodates—but does not cease—its symptomatic functioning in response to a therapeutic intervention. Thus, the family may have been symptomatic in one way, but it may now be symptomatic in another way. (Watzlawick, Weakland, & Fisch, 1974) [See *cybernetics, second order change*]

FOLIE A DEUX

An early expression which meant "the madness of two." In family therapy it refers to a delusional system in which two family members, typically a marital dyad or a parent-child dyad, collude in such a way that it is not possible to determine which of them is psychotic and which is not. It is an example of psychosis shared at a systems level. (Oberndorf, 1934)

FUSION

A concept from *Family of Origin Therapy* that describes the tendency of one family member to become so emotionally attached to another that one's own self-identity and personal boundaries become blurred with the other person. It is the opposite of *differentiation of self*. (Bowen, 1978) [See *differentiation of self, Family of Origin Therapy*]

GENDER ROLES

A term describing socially prescribed roles which delineate different behaviors assumed appropriate for men and women. A feminist critique would suggest that women's roles have limited their access to resources and behaviors in both the family and larger social systems. (Ariel, 1999; Walters, Carter, Papp, & Silverstein, 1988) [See *Feminist Family Therapy, gender sensitivity*]

GENDER SENSITIVITY

A concept, developed by Lynn Hoffman, to recommend that the concern for gender issues become a significant part of the theory and practice of family therapy. For the family therapist, this necessitates an understanding of the effects of differential socialization for both genders and the goal of providing opportunities for both partners to choose "voices" and roles that may differ from those prescribed by the larger social system. (Ariel, 1999; Hoffman, 1990) [See *Feminist Family Therapy, gender roles*]

GENERAL SYSTEMS THEORY

The theory, developed by physicist Ludwig von Bertalanffy, which first defined the relationship of objects, or individuals, within biologic, economic, or physical systems. This theory became the conceptual foundation for much of family systems theory and therapy. (Von Bertalanffy, 1974, 1968)

GENOGRAM

A diagram (See Figure 4) of extended family relationships which includes at least three generations. For the family therapist, a genogram provides a visual map of family *structure* and recurring patterns, as well as critical events such as births, marriages, divorces and deaths. (DeMaria, Weeks, & Hof, 1999; McGoldrick, Gerson, & Shellenberger, 1999; McGoldrick & Gerson, 1985; Guerin, 1976) [See *family map*]

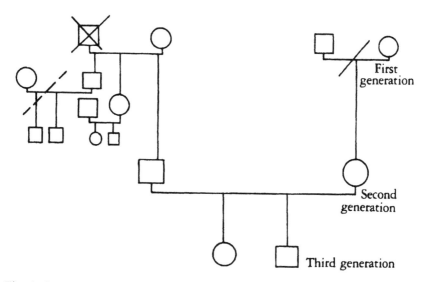

Fig. 4. Genogram

GOOD OBJECTS/BAD OBJECTS

Terms, which evolved from *object relations theory* and the psychiatric symptoms of the Borderline Personality Disorder, that describe for family therapists a process of emotional *splitting* which occurs within a family system (as compared to an individual) whereby one family member is perceived as gratifying or "good" and another is perceived as misbehaving or "bad." (Everett & Everett, 1997; Everett, Halperin, Volgy, & Wissler, 1989; Framo, 1982) [See *borderline process, splitting*]

HIERARCHY

A concept from *Structural Family Therapy* which defines the way leadership and power is organized within family systems and how the decision making process may be based on such family variables as age and gender. (Minuchin, 1974) [See *Structural Family Therapy*]

HOMEOSTASIS

A concept from systems theory that describes the dynamic state of a system where one or more variables are stable and balanced. For example, in a family system, the interplay between marital conflict, a child's asthma attacks, and family harmony while the parents care for their sick child may be both stable and repetitive, and, thus, homeostatic. A family therapist may intervene to disrupt the homeostasis (*perturbation*) in an effort to achieve *first* or *second order change*. (Dell, 1984, 1982) [See *first-order change, perturbation, second order change*]

HYPOTHESIZING

A clinical process in family systems assessment and treatment where available information on the family is used by the therapist to form an hypothesis regarding clinical issues which can be tested and validated in the subsequent family interviews. (Palazolli, Boscolo, Cecchin, & Prata, 1980; Cecchin, 1987)

IDENTIFIED PATIENT

A term developed early in family therapy to designate the family member who displays the symptoms and for whom therapy has been sought. The identified patient often may be labeled by the family as "crazy" or "sick." (Satir, 1967)

INCONGRUOUS POWER HIERARCHIES

A concept which describes an ongoing imbalance of power in a marital dyad that generates a constant state of tension. These patterns are inherently unstable and represent a disparity between the apparent structure of reality in the system and the actual interactional dynamics. For example, one partner may have the higher overt status but the other partner may have more control and responsibility in certain areas. (Schnarch, 1991) [See *hierarchy*]

INTERGENERATIONAL LOYALTIES

A concept (See Figure 5), developed by Ivan Boszormenyi-Nagy, which describes a foundation of emotional commitments and obligations experienced by family members toward their families of origin. Two types of loyalties are defined: vertical loyalties are those embedded in one's early childhood roles and family of origin attachments; horizontal loyalties occur at marriage with the development of new attachments to an adult partner. (Boszormenyi-Nagy & Spark, 1973) [See *Contextual Family Therapy, multigenerational transmission process*]

INTERLOCKING PATHOLOGIES

An early definition of the complex and multiple levels of clinical dynamics that occur within family systems (i.e., intrapsychic and interpersonal). Ackerman (1956) defined three clinical dimensions: (1) the group dynamics of the family; (2) the emotional integration of an individual within the family; and (3) the internal organization and development of each individual member. Ackerman (1956) believed that a family therapist needed to analyze all three levels to gain a complete clinical assessment.

"I" POSITION

A concept from *Family of Origin Therapy* which refers to the ability of a family member to take a position based on the person's own thinking and self-identity and to maintain it in the face of emotional pressure to change from other family members—a process of *differentiation* within the family system. (Bowen, 1978) [See *differentiation, Family of Origin Therapy*]

ISOMORPHISM

A concept from systems theory that describes when certain structural aspects of one system match structural aspects of another system, i.e., "similar shapes." The family therapist may seek to match therapeutic role or style with that of the clinical family system. (Keeney, 1983; Bateson, 1972) [See *isomorphic intervention*]

ISOMORPHIC INTERVENTION

A clinical intervention which addresses simultaneously problems at multiple systemic levels: i.e., intrapsychic issues, interaction between members, and broader family system patterns. For the family therapist, it is more effective to direct relevant interventions at all of these levels than just one. (Schnarch,

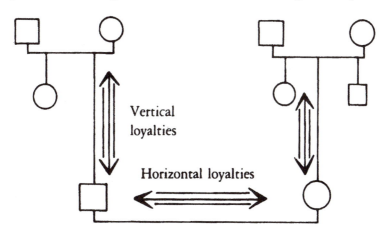

Fig. 5. Intergenerational loyalties

1991) [See *interlocking pathologies, isomorphism*]

JOINING

A clinical process from *Structural Family Therapy* which describes the therapist's role of entering and establishing rapport with members of the family system. Together with *accommodation,* these processes describe the primary ways by which the family therapist develops a therapeutic system with the family. (Minuchin, 1974) [See *accommodation, Structural Family Therapy*]

LINEAR CAUSALITY

A concept from systems theory that describes a nonreciprocal relationship which exists between sequential events such that the initial event causes the second event but the second event does not reciprocally act upon the first event (Goldenberg & Goldenberg, 1996; Nichols & Schwartz, 1998; Wynne, 1988, Dell, 1985; Hoffman, 1981; Bateson, 1972) [See *circular causality, epistemology*]

LIVE SUPERVISION

A clinical education method, utilized extensively in family therapy training, which enhances the learning potential for the student-therapist by utilizing immediate supervisory feedback during the process of the clinical interview. The supervisor, or a team of supervisors and colleagues, may offer consultation to the student-therapist by use of such methods as a "bug-in-the-ear," telephonic conversation, and live discussion with the student-therapist while the clinical session is in progress. (Liddle, 1991; Schwartz, Liddle, & Breunlin 1988; Haley, 1976; Montalvo, 1973)

MANAGED CARE

A health care system in which third-party payers regulate and control the cost, quality, and terms of health care services, including family therapy treatment.

MARITAL CONTRACTS

A concept, developed by Clifford Sager, that describes a set of expectations and promises, both conscious and unconscious, that each partner brings into the marriage. The family therapist often helps couples negotiate dissimilar expectations into a more integrative, joint expectation. (Sager, 1981, 1976)

MATE SELECTION

A process described in family theory by which an individual chooses a partner for marriage. This process includes sociological, demographic, and ecological variables, as well as conscious and unconscious elements. (Framo, 1982; Winch, 1954) [See *complementarity*]

MEDICAL FAMILY THERAPY

A clinical approach based on *collaboration* with physicians and other health care professionals in the treatment of family systems and their members. Family therapists provide an integrative orientation with other providers in collaboratively treating health care issues in a family system. (Seaburn, Lorenz, Gunn, Gawinski, & Mauksch, 1996; McDaniel, Hepworth, & Doherty, 1992) [See *collaboration, ecosystemic perspective*]

METACOMMUNICATION

A concept that describes an implicit and often nonverbal message which addresses the intent of a verbal statement. A metamessage may support the primary statement or contradict it, as occurs in a *double-bind*. For example, a mother may tell her child to eat her soup and then hand her a spoon (her metacommunication). Handing of the spoon to the child is consistent with her verbal message. However, if the mother takes the soup away, having told the child to eat it, her metacommunication contradicts her primary statement. Without further clarification, this latter example would constitute a *paradox*. However, if the mother places an ice cube in the soup to cool it and returns it to the child the apparent paradox is clarified. (Bateson, 1972) [See *double-bind, paradox*]

MIMESIS

A form of *accommodation* and *joining* from *Structural Family Therapy* whereby the family therapist mirrors (imitates) the family's style, tempo, and affect. (Minuchin, 1974) [See *accommodation, joining, Structural Family Therapy*]

MORPHOGENESIS

A concept from systems theory which describes the tendency of a system to evolve and to change its structure. (Hoffman, 1973) [See *morphostasis*]

MORPHOSTASIS

A concept from systems theory which describes the tendency of a system to retain its basic organization (i.e., to remain the same). (Hoffman, 1973) [See *morphogenesis*]

MULTIGENERATIONAL TRANSMISSION PROCESS

A concept utilized in a variety of family systems models to describe the transmission of certain roles, beliefs, values, myths, interactional behaviors, and structural patterns across multiple generations. (Bowen, 1978; Boszormenyi-Nagy & Spark, 1973) [See *Contextual Family Therapy, Family of Origin Therapy, intergenerational loyalties*]

MULTIPLE FAMILY THERAPY

A clinical method in which a variety of families, often up to five to six, are seen together in a joint group session to focus on presenting problems and family behaviors. The method was developed by Peter Laqueur who felt that family members learned indirectly, i.e., by observing how well or poorly others accomplished a similar task, such as fathering. (Laqueur, 1973)

MULTIPLE IMPACT THERAPY

A clinical method using a team of family therapists who interview family members in varying combinations of subsystems over an intensive period of two to three days. The intensity of this approach is designed to dissipate resistances and to give the team a broader range of information from which to make interventions. (MacGregor, McDonald, & Goolishian, 1964)

NARRATIVE FAMILY THERAPY

A clinical model, developed by Michael White and David Epston, which focuses on helping family systems to develop positive and successful "life stories" (*alternative stories*) which replace their former focus on pathological patterns. (White, 1997, 1992; Freedman & Combs, 1996; White & Epston, 1990) [See *alternative story, dominant narrative*]

NEGENTROPY

A concept from systems theory which describes the emergence of a system's organizational patterns which leads to knowledge about the system. This concept is the opposite (or negative) of *entropy*. (Bateson, 1972) [See *entropy*]

NETWORK THERAPY

A clinical method, developed by Ross Speck and Carolyn Attneave, in which resources throughout and external to the family system are recruited and involved in the family therapy process to assist the family in working on the problem. These resources may include extended family members, neighbors, other health care or mental health providers, work colleagues, children's playmates, teachers, etc. As many as 50 to100 participants may be involved in a therapy session. (Speck & Attneave, 1973)

OBJECT RELATIONS

An early psychodynamic theory which described the internalized images of one's self and others that are based on early parent–child interactions. These images may become the model for subsequent interpersonal relations in one's family of origin, mate selection, family of procreation, and other intimate relationships. (Nichols & Schwartz, 1998; Scharff & Scharff, 1987; Nichols & Everett, 1986; Framo, 1982; Dicks, 1967) [See *borderline process, family projection process, good/bad objects, projective identification, splitting*]

OPEN SYSTEMS

A term from *general systems theory* that refers to systems which are continuously open to the exchange of information from it's environment (*feedback*). Living systems are, by definition, open systems. As used by family therapists, the terms *"open system"* and *"closed system"* are metaphors referring to the extent to which a family is "open" to new information and, hence, susceptible to change. (Dell, 1985, 1984) [See *boundaries, closed systems, feedback loops, general systems theory*]

ORDINAL POSITION

A concept (See Figure 6) that defines the relative birth order position of each family member within one's sibling subsystem, e.g., oldest daughter, youngest son. The impact of this member's position may affect factors of personality

Oldest-youngest mate selection

Fig. 6. Ordinal position: potential influence on mate selection

formation and role development within the family of origin, and influence subsequent adult mate selection. For example, the youngest sister of an older brother may select as a mate a male who was an older brother; reciprocally the eldest brother with a younger sister may select a female mate who was a younger sister. (Hoopes & Harper, 1987; Toman, 1976) [See *family maps, genograms*]

ORGANIZATION

The relationship among the components of a system which are both necessary and sufficient for defining the nature and identity of the system. For example, diffuse internal *boundaries* and high levels of reactivity among members are family dynamics necessary to define a system as *enmeshing*. If the organization of a system changes, then the system will become a different type. (Whitchurch & Constantine, 1993; Maturana, 1978) (See *boundaries, enmeshing family systems, disengaging family systems, second order change, structure*)

OVERFUNCTIONING/ UNDERFUNCTIONING POSITIONS

These concepts from *Family of Origin Therapy* describe reciprocal roles within a family system. For example, an underfunctioning member may be dependent on a partner for caretaking or to assume responsibility for activities one is unable or unwilling to do. An overfunctioning member may feel responsible for the emotional well-being of the partner and even act to compensate for real or imagined deficits in the functioning of the other. While this relationship may assist family functioning when levels of stress are low, increases in stress may push both members to polarized behaviors. A parent may assume an overfunctioning role which maintains a child at an excessively dependent and underfunctioning role. (Kerr & Bowen, 1988)

PARADOX

A clinical intervention where the family therapist offers a message to the family which is both internally inconsistent and contradictory (e.g., a *double-bind* message). The multiple or contradictory meanings that are presented to a family have the intent of challenging rigid perceptions or *perturbing* and unbalancing the system. The family therapist expects the family to resist the directive in a manner that change may occur. For example, a therapist may *prescribe* an escalation of the family's symptoms or explain to the family that it is best not to get better now. (Watzlawick & Weakland, 1977; Haley, 1963) [See *double-bind, perturbation, prescribing the symptom, Strategic Family Therapy, unbalancing*]

PARENTIFICATION

A family system dynamic where a child is assigned a caretaking role for one or both parents, and often for the siblings, too. This designated child assumes excessive responsibility in a pseudo-adult role by emotionally and/or physically caring for either a weak parent (or sibling) or a vulnerable parental marriage. This role diffuses marital stress and reciprocally reinforces the power of the child in the family. There is often an associated effect of sibling rivalry. In some family systems the parentified child may be more vulnerable to incidents of incest or physical abuse. (Boszormenyi-Nagy & Spark, 1973) [See *scapegoating*]

PERTURBATION

A clinical intervention in which the family therapist acts upon the system to produce a structural change or accommodation. The system must respond to and compensate for the intervention. This is often intended to *unbalance* the system in order to increase the potential for change. (Maturana, 1978) [See *tickling the defenses, unbalancing*]

POSITIVE CONNOTATION

A clinical intervention to *reframe* family behaviors so that they maintain a balance or cohesion within the system. The intervention is focused on attributing positive intentions to problematic sequences or roles, and reflects elements of the *homeostatic* pattern in the family. The focus of the reframe is not limited to the *identified patient* alone, but may include the family in general. (Palazzoli, Boscolo, Cecchin, & Prata, 1978) [See *homeostasis, identified patient, reframing*]

POSTMODERN THINKING

A theoretical movement that emerged in the family therapy field in the 1970s and 1980s. The modernist approach has been criticized for ignoring issues such as gender, ethnicity, and the impact of larger systems, such as political and economic forces, on the family. The postmodern approach believes that these factors are critical and need to be incorporated in the conceptualization process. While modernism encouraged allegiance to a single model of therapy, the postmodern approach is more eclectic and tries to incorporate ideas outside family therapy. *Constructivism,* an aspect of the postmodern movement, views reality as subjective, and family processes as interpretive, not fact. Postmodern thinking looks at different perspectives, blends theory and therapy, and examines macro-processes. (Hoffman, 1992; Doherty, 1991) [See *constructivism*]

PRAGMATICS 1st

A complement to *aesthetics,* wholism pragmatics refers to a reductionistic stance in which the focus in family therapy is on resolving the presenting problem while generally ignoring the larger gestalt in which the presenting problem exists. A pragmatic therapist is more concerned with techniques that work than with remaining sensitive to holistic patterns. (Keeney, 1983; Keeney & Sprenkle, 1982) [See *aesthetics*]

Pragmatics also describes the behavioral effects of communications. (Nichols & Schwartz, 1998)

PRESCRIBING THE SYMPTOM

A clinical intervention that takes the form of *paradox* and *double bind*. A therapist instructs a family member to enact a symptomatic behavior, which creates the expectation that an "involuntary" behavior will become voluntary. The person may acknowledge that the behavior is involuntary or simply give up the symptom. An example of prescribing the symptom is telling an overprotective mother to take better care of her child. (Watzlawick, Beavin, & Jackson, 1967) [See *paradox, perturbation, Strategic Family Therapy*]

PROJECTIVE IDENTIFICATION

A concept from psychodynamic theory which defines a defensive mechanism in individuals. In family therapy it represents an interactional pattern in family systems in which aspects or parts of a member's personality that one feels are unacceptable are projected onto another member of the family. A reciprocal process causes the other family member to accept the projection and act in accordance with it. For example, a father may find his own aggressive feelings unacceptable. He may project them onto an adolescent, covertly provoking the child into aggressive behaviors. The child then "owns" the projection and acts aggressively, while the father calmly berates the child without having to feel that the aggression is a part of himself. (Everett & Everett, 1997; Zinner & Shapiro, 1989; Everett, Halperin, Volgy, & Wissler, 1989; Framo, 1982; Skynner, 1981, 1976) [See *borderline process, splitting*]

PSEUDO-HOSTILITY

A family dynamic used as a defense for the system where hostility and conflict camouflage underlying dysfunctional elements. (Nichols & Schwartz, 1998) [See *pseudo-mutuality*]

PSEUDO-MUTUALITY

An early clinical concept that described a family's presentation to the family therapist as an outward picture of intimacy and harmony which served to camouflage underlying conflicts and dysfunctions. Family therapists will recognize this as a form of resistance to one's attempts to *join* or intervene with the family system. (Wynne, Ryckoff, Day, & Hirsch, 1958) [See *joining, pseudo-hostility*]

POWER

A concept that defines a family member's ability to influence or control circumstances and events. Such a role in a family is determined largely by the distribution of resources held by members of the system. (Carter & McGoldrick, 1999) [See *gender sensitivity*]

PROCESS

A concept from family systems theory which describes the repetitions, redundancies, and predictabilities of a family system that appear clinically in a sequence of actions and interactions among family members. This is often contrasted with the "content," or verbal information that is available from a family. (Nichols & Everett, 1986)

PUNCTUATION

The family systems dynamic by which members perceive and mark distinctions in their interactions with one another. Each partner believes that what she or he says was caused by what the other had said. For example, a husband and wife in conflict may report: "She nags me so I withdraw" and "He withdraws so I nag him." These are different punctuations of the same interactional process. (Keeney, 1983; Bateson, 1972; Watzlawick, Beavin, & Jackson, 1967)

QUID PRO QUO

A contract between two individuals in which each gives to the other a certain favor or recognition and receives in turn a similar favor of relatively equal value. Family therapists often see these as a subtle rules within families that are the result of bargaining to protect sensitive issues or *secrets*. (Jacobson & Holtzworth-Munroe, 1986; Jackson, 1965)

In *Behavior Family Therapy,* quid pro quo contracts may be negotiated as a means of changing behavior patterns in accordance with each partner's wishes. (Jacobson & Holtzworth-Munroe, 1986; Jacobson & Margolin, 1979; Greenberg, 1977) [See *Behavioral Family Therapy*]

RECIPROCITY

A concept from family systems theory that describes interactions between family members where the behavior of one person "dovetails" or "fits" together with that of another in a *complementary* fashion. For example, if one partner is overtly aggressive in a relationship, the other partner may respond reciprocally, in a submissive manner. However, the partner's response may be in a covert or passive-aggressive form that may in turn provoke the other partner into more aggression. [See *complementarity*]

RECIPROCAL STRUCTURAL COUPLING

A concept from systems theory which describes the organizational closure that is attained by a system when circularity is achieved. For example, the disruptive behavior of an adolescent may trigger reciprocal behaviors in the other siblings, which then recursively loop back to trigger amplified or modified behaviors in the adolescent. The result is an organized, stable system. (Dell, 1982) [See *circular process, feedback loops*]

REFLECTING TEAM

A clinical intervention in family therapy that is employed both as a training method and a consultation method. Reflecting teams are supervisors and/or colleagues who observe the live family therapy process (usually behind a one-way mirror). They may intervene in the clinical process by sending, calling, or walking messages into the session. The messages may offer observations, support, or opposition to the therapist's role with the family. (Kaslow, Kaslow, & Farber, 1999; Anderson, 1990; Papp, 1980) [See *live supervision*]

REFRAMING

A clinical intervention which challenges a family's perception of a symptom or conflict both by *relabeling* it (such as in a *positive connotation*) and altering the context in which it is perceived. For example, the "illness" of an anorectic child is reframed in a new context which defines the child being disobedient and disrespectful to the parents. This not only redefines the behavior from illness to disobedience, but it also defines the behavior in relation to the family system itself. (Minuchin, 1974; Watzlawick, Weakland, & Fisch, 1974) [See *relabeling, Structural Family Therapy*]

RELABELING

A clinical intervention where symptoms are restated or redefined in interpersonal terms instead of with the focus of a symptom on an individual member. This intervention challenges the family's perception of the symptoms or behaviors. For example, an adolescent's behavior, described by the parents as rebellious and antagonistic, may be relabeled more normatively as "growing up" experiences. (Minuchin, 1974) [See *reframing*]

RESTRUCTURING

A clinical intervention from *Structural Family Therapy* which describes interventions that are directed toward challenging and altering the family system's structure, e.g., strengthening the boundaries around the spousal subsystem. (Minuchin, 1974) [See *perturbation, Structural Family Therapy*]

ROLES

A concept from family theory that describes images and/or positions with characteristic behaviors that are assigned to specific members to perform certain functions within a family system. They may represent normative positions such as a parent or a child, or dysfunctional positions such as a *parentified* child or a *scapegoat*. (Minuchin, 1974, Ackerman, 1958) [See *parentification, scapegoating*]

RUBBER FENCE

A concept used as a metaphor to describe an unstable but continuous family *boundary* which may stretch to include supportive and positive influences and then may contract to exclude that which is perceived by the family as threatening. Wynne observed that families with this dynamic appeared to accommodate to the family therapist's interventions, but later returned to their former habitual configuration and organization. (Wynne, Ryckoff, Day, & Hirsch, 1958) [See *boundaries*]

RUNAWAY

A concept from systems theory describing a system which responds to positive *feedback* in such a way that dysfunctions and errors are reinforced and escalated, causing the system to be moved further "off-track." This is in contrast to systems receiving negative feedback by which they become more self-correcting. (Watzlawick, Beavin, & Jackson, 1967) (See *deviation amplification, feedback loops*)

SCAPEGOATING

A family system dynamic that describes the process by which a family designates a member to carry and act out the stress and dysfunction for other members or subsystems of the family. For example, often a child is designated to carry this stress and it may be displayed in depressive symptoms or delinquent behaviors. A family therapist may see a child acting out due to underlying conflicts in the parent's marriage. (Vogel & Bell, 1960) (See *parentification*)

SCULPTING

A clinical intervention, adapted by Peggy Papp from psychodrama, in which a family member is asked to depict a view of the emotional closeness or distance among the members of a family system. A family therapist will ask the member to arrange (direct) family members physically in certain locations to represent their roles and alliances in the family. The resulting tableau represents that member's symbolic view of their family's dynamics and interactions. (Papp, 1980, Papp, Silverstein, & Carter, 1973; Duhl, Kantor, & Duhl, 1973)

SECOND-ORDER CHANGE

A concept from systems theory that describes the process of change in a system which alters the fundamental organization of the system. In family therapy a symptomatic system can be said to undergo second order change when a therapeutic intervention fundamentally disrupts the pattern of symptomatic interaction so that it ceases. The family's previous organization, which reinforced the symptomatic pattern, is replaced by a different organization. (Watzlawick & Weakland, 1977; Watzlawick, Weakland, & Fisch, 1974) (See *cybernetics, first order change, organization*)

SIDE TAKING

A clinical intervention in which the family therapist deliberately "sides" with one member or a certain position over another in the family. The goal is to unbalance the dysfunctional aspect of the family system so that change can occur. Zuk felt that this intervention forced the family into changing as a way of avoiding the power and influence of the therapist. (Zuk, 1971) [See *perturbation, unbalancing*]

SOLUTION-FOCUSED FAMILY THERAPY

A clinical model that identifies solutions to current and specific problems described by clients imposing as little change as possible. The model suggests that even slight change can have lasting effects in other areas of a family's life and treatment is considered ended and successful when the presenting problem has been eliminated. (De Shazer, 1982, 1985, 1988) [See *Brief Family Therapy*)

SPLITTING

A concept from *object relations* theory which defines a defensive maneuver whereby an individual "splits" the "good" from the "bad" in an external object and internalizes this split perception. In family therapy it has been used to describe an interactional dynamic within family systems where positive and negative feelings, and thoughts are split and experienced in isolation from one another. This behavior distorts the family's perception and experience of reality in such a way that the family tends to view internal as well as external experiences in terms of "black and white" issues without regard for the complexities of the total reality. For example, in the systemic *borderline process* a family splits their perceptions of two children and designates one as "good" and another as "bad." (Becvar & Becvar, 2000; Everett & Everett, 1997; Everett, Halperin, Volgy, & Wissler, 1989; Skynner, 1981, 1976) (See *borderline process, good/bad objects, object relations theory, projective identification*)

STRATEGIC FAMILY THERAPY

A clinical model in which the family therapist designs interventions focused on specific problems. The model uses a *cybernetic* view which recognizes that symptoms in a family are perpetuated in a recursive sequence such that a "solution" may involve maintenance and continuation of the actual problem. The goals of most strategic interventions are to induce *second-order change* in the family system. (Madanes, 1984, 1981; Haley, 1963) [See *paradox, perturbation, prescribing the symptom*]

STRUCTURAL DETERMINISM

A concept from systems theory which defines the potential range of change that a system can tolerate (e.g., in response to a *perturbation*) without a loss of identity. The structure sets limits to how a system can respond and what changes it can make. (Becvar & Becvar, 2000; Efran, Lukens & Lukens, 1988) [See *organization, perturbation, restructuring, structure*]

STRUCTURAL FAMILY THERAPY

A clinical model, developed by Salvador Minuchin, based on identifying the internal organization of subsystems and boundaries of a family system, and the manner in which these structural elements define interactional patterns and behaviors. (Aponte & Van Deusen, 1991; Minuchin & Fishman, 1981; Minuchin, 1974) [See *accommodation, enactment, joining, maintenance, mimesis, reframing, relabeling, restructuring, tracking, unbalancing*]

STRUCTURE

A concept from systems theory that defines the components, and the relationship among these components, which define the organization of a system. A structure may undergo a wide range of changes (i.e., *first order changes*) which will not alter the underlying organization of the system. (Maturana, 1978; Minuchin, 1974) (See *first order change, organization, second order change, structural determinism*]

SUBSYSTEMS

A concept from family systems theory (See Figure 7) which describes the basic structural units within the nuclear family system—spousal, parent-child, sibling. (Minuchin, 1974)

SYMBOLIC-EXPERIENTIAL FAMILY THERAPY

A clinical model, developed by Carl Whitaker, which stresses the immediacy of human interactions within the family system while focusing on the family's underlying symbolic representations of their impulses, irrationalities, and "craziness." Family therapists working from this model participate actively and personally in the therapy process, using their own affect, fantasies, spontaneity, creativity and present-centeredness to touch the family's underlying issues and

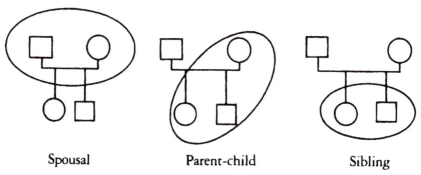

Fig. 7. Subsystems

help remove emotional obstacles in the system. (Whitaker, 1989, 1982; Whitaker & Bumberry, 1988; Napier & Whitaker, 1978)

SYMMETRICAL

A concept that describes a relationship in which the family members (e.g., spouses) have relatively equal status and power. This relationship type may display greater conflict than *complementary* patterns, because the relatively equal status of the partners can cause disputes to escalate circularly leading to a greater disruption. (Bateson, 1972, 1979, 1936) [See *complementary*]

SYSTEM

A concept that defines the basic set of units or elements interconnected in a consistent relationship or interactional stance such that whatever affects one part of the system will affect other parts. Systems can be open or closed, depending on their receptiveness to environmental information. (Nichols & Everett, 1986; Steinglass, 1978; von Bertalanffy, 1974, 1968) [See *boundaries, subsystems*]

SYSTEMS CONSULTATION

An approach in which systemic principles used in working with families can be applied to other contexts and larger systems, such as corporate organizations or small businesses. The focus is on the systematic aspects of the organizational environment rather than specific problems. The consultant's/therapist's goal is to find ways of allowing new information to enter the system so that change may occur. (Campbell, Draper, & Huffington, 1989; Wynne, McDaniel, & Weber, 1987)

TICKLING THE DEFENSES

A historic term, coined by Nathan Ackerman, to describe the process by which the family therapist moves in and out of the system, making observations that are provocative and pushing the family to its limits. This was the term Ackerman used to describe the struggle for control of the family system. (Ackerman, 1982, 1958) [See *battle for initiative, battle for structure, joining, perturbation*]

TRACKING

An *accommodation* technique whereby the family therapist follows the direction and content of a family's communication and behavior, and encourages its continuance. Tracking follows the evolution of themes and content within a system. (Minuchin, 1974) [See *accommodation*]

TRANSFERENCE

A concept in psychotherapy which defined the personal and/or "distorted" feelings which may develop in a client toward their therapist. In family therapy it describes distortions that are experienced by family members in the therapeutic context and directed toward the therapist or other family members. A collective transference that is experienced by the whole family system may also occur. (Framo, 1992, 1982) [See *countertransference*]

TRIANGLING

A family dynamic (See Figure 8) describing the process whereby a third family member is introduced into a dyadic relationship to balance either uncomfortable intimacy or a certain level of conflict or distance experienced by the dyad. The process provides balance and stability to the system, but may also reinforce dysfunctional interactions. For example, a *scapegoated* or *parentified* child may have been triangled into the parental dyad. (Nichols & Everett, 1986; Bowen, 1978) [See *parentification, scapegoating*]

TRIANGULATION

A family dynamic, often represented by a rigid triadic relationship between two parents and a child, in which each parent demands that the child side with him or her in a conflict. The child may become paralyzed because, no matter what response is given, he or she will be perceived by one of the parents as betraying that parent's expectations.

This term can also refer to any triad in which the conflict between two members pulls in a third member in such a way that the latter is immobilized in a loyalty conflict. (Minuchin, 1974) [See *triangling*]

UNBALANCING

A clinical intervention from *Structural Family Therapy* where the family therapist interferes with a dysfunctional transactional in the system by adding more force or emphasis to a certain behavior or role. The goal is to interfere with the equilibrium of the system which maintains the problem. For example, a therapist might *join* with one family member in order to force other members to interact in a *reciprocal,* or even *runaway* manner. (Minuchin, 1974) [See *perturbation, restructuring, runaway, side-taking, Structural Family Therapy*)

UNDIFFERENTIATED EGO MASS

A concept, developed by Murray Bowen, to describe a lack of *differentiation of self* observed in family members. Stress in a family system can lead to a diffusion of internal *boundaries* and a blurring and confusion of family members' identities. (Bowen, 1978) [See *fusion*]

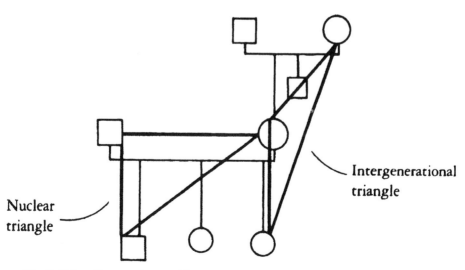

Fig. 8. Triangling: nuclear and intergenerational

BIBLIOGRAPHY

Ackerman, N. (1956). Interlocking pathology in family relationships. In S. Redo & G. Daniels (Eds.) *Changing concepts of psychoanalytic medicine.* New York: Grune & Stratton.

Ackerman, N. (1958). *The psychodynamics of family life.* New York: Basic Books.

Ackerman, N. (1982). *The strength of family therapy.* Selected Papers of Nathan W. Ackerman. D. Bloch & R. Simon (Eds.) New York: Brunner/Mazel.

American Association for Marriage and Family Therapy. (1999). *AAMFT code of ethics.* Washington, D.C.

Anderson, H. (1995). Collaborative language systems: Toward a postmodern therapy. In R.H. Mikesell, D.D. Lusterman, & S.H. McDaniel (Eds.), *Integrating family therapy: Handbook of family psychology and systems theory* (pp. 27–44). Washington, DC: APA.

Anderson, H. & Goolishian, H. (1992). The client is the expert: A not-knowing approach to therapy. In S. McNamee & K.J. Gergen (Eds.), *Therapy as social construction* (pp. 25–39). Newbury Park, CA: Sage.

Anderson, S., & Bagarozzi, D. (1989). *Family myths: Psychotherapy implications.* New York: The Haworth Press.

Anderson, T. (Ed.), (1990). *The reflecting team.* Kent, U.K.: Borgmann Publishing Limited.

Aponte, H. (1980). Family therapy and the community. In Margaret Gibbs, J. R. Lachenmeyer, & Janet Sigal (Eds.), *Community Psychology,* (pp. 311–333). New York: Gardener Press.

Aponte, H. S., & VanDeusen, J. M. (1991). Structural family therapy. In A. S. Gurman & D.P. Kniskern (Eds.), *Handbook of family therapy,* Vol. I (pp. 310–360). New York: Brunner/Mazel.

Ariel, S. (1999). *Culturally competent family therapy: A general model.* Westport, CT: Praeger.

Auerswald, E. (1968). Interdisciplinary versus ecological approach. *Family Process, 1,* 205–215.

Bateson, G. (1936). *Naven.* Cambridge, England: Cambridge University Press.

Bateson, G. (1972). *Steps to an ecology of mind.* New York: Ballantine.

Bateson, G. (1979). *Mind and nature: A necessary unity.* New York: Dutton.

Bateson, G., Jackson, D., Haley, J., & Weakland, J. (1956). Toward a theory of schizophrenia. *Behavioral Science, 1,* 251–254.

Beavers, R. (1977). *Psychotherapy and growth.* New York: Brunner/Mazel.

Becvar, D. S., & Becvar, R. J. (2000). *Family therapy: A systematic integration.* Boston, MA: Allyn & Bacon.

Berg, I. K., & DeShazer, S. (1993). Making numbers talk: Language in therapy. In S. Friedman (Ed.), *The new language of change* (pp. 5–24). New York: Guilford.

Boszormenyi-Nagy, I., & Spark, G. (1973). *Invisible loyalties: Reciprocity in intergenerational family therapy.* New York: Harper & Row.

Boszormenyi-Nagy, I., & Krasner, B. R. (1986). *Between give and take: A clinical guide to contextual therapy.* New York: Brunner/Mazel.

Bowen, M. (1978). *Family therapy in clinical practice.* New York: Aronson.

Brown, J. (1997). Circular questioning: An introductory guide. *Australian and New Zealand Journal of Family Therapy, 18,* 109–114.

Campbell, D., Draper, R., & Huffington, C. (1989). *A systemic approach to consultation.* London: Karnac Books.

Campbell, D., Draper, R., & Crutchley, E. (1991). The Milan approach to family therapy. In A. S. Gurman & D. P. Kniskern (Eds.) *Handbook of family therapy,* (pp. 325–361). New York: Brunner/Mazel.

Carter, B., & McGoldrick, M. (1989). *The changing family life cycle: A framework for therapy* (2nd ed.). Boston: Allyn & Bacon.

Carter, B., & McGoldrick, M. (1999). *The expanded family life cycle: A framework for family therapy* (3rd ed.). Boston: Allyn & Bacon.

Cecchin, G. (1987). Hypothesizing, circularity, and neutrality revisited: An invitation to curiosity. *Family Process, 26,* 405–413.

Crosby, J. (Ed.) (1989). *When one wants out and the other doesn't: Doing therapy with polarized couples.* New York: Brunner/Mazel.

DeMaria, R., Weeks, G., & Hof, L. (1999). *Focused genograms: Intergenerational assessment of individual, couples, and families.* New York: Brunner/Mazel

DeShazer, S. (1982). *Patterns of brief family therapy.* New York: Guilford Press.

DeShazer, S. (1985). *Keys to solution in brief therapy.* New York: W.W. Norton.

DeShazer, S. (1988). *Clues: Investigating solutions in brief therapy.* New York: W. W. Norton.

Dell, P. (1982). Beyond homeostasis: Toward a concept of coherence. *Family Process, 21,* 21–41.

Dell, P. (1984). Why family therapy should go beyond homeostasis: A Kuhnian reply to Tyano, Carel and Ariel. *Journal of Marital and Family Therapy, 10,* 351–356.

Dell, P. (1985). Understanding Bateson and Maturana: Toward a biological foundation for the social sciences. *Journal of Marital and Family Therapy, 11,* 1–20.

Dicks, H. (1967). *Marital tensions.* New York: Basic Books.

Doherty, W. J., (1991). Family therapy goes postmodern. *The Family Therapy Networker, 15,* 36–42.

Duhl, F. J., Kantor, D., & Duhl, B. S. (1973). Learning space, and action in family therapy: A primer of sculpture. In D.A. Bloch (Ed.), *Techniques of family psychotherapy: A primer.* New York: Grune & Stratton.

Efran, J. S. Lukens R. J., & Lukens, M. D. (1988). Constructivism: What's in it for you. *The Family Therapy Networker, 12,* 27–35.

Epstein N. B., Bishop, D. S., & Levin, S. (1978). The McMaster model of family functioning. *Journal of Marriage and Family Counseling, 4,* 19–31.

Epstein, N., & Schlesinger, S. E. (1996).

Cognitive-behavioral treatment of family problems. In M. Reinecke, F. M. Dattilio, & A. Freeman (Eds.), *Casebook of cognitive-behavior therapy with children and adolescents.* New York: Guilford.

Erickson, S. & McKnight, M. (2000). *A practitioner's guide to mediation.* New York: Wiley.

Erickson, S., & Erickson, M. (1988). *Family mediation casebook.* New York: Brunner/Mazel.

Everett, C. A. (1985). *Divorce mediation: Perspectives on the field.* New York: Haworth.

Everett, C. A., Halperin, S., Volgy, S., & Wissler, A. (1989). *Treating the borderline family: A systemic approach.* Boston: Allyn & Bacon.

Everett, C.A., & Volgy, S. (1991). Treating divorce in family-therapy practice. In A. S. Gurman and D. P. Kniskern (Eds.). *Handbook of family therapy,* Vol. II (pp. 508–524). New York: Brunner/Mazel.

Everett, C. A., & Everett, S. V. (1994). *Healthy divorce.* San Francisco: Jossey-Bass.

Everett, C. A., & Volgy Everett, S. V. (1997). *Short term family therapy with borderline patients.* Galena, IL: Geist & Russell.

Falicov, C. (1988). Learning to think culturally. In H. Liddle, D. Breunlin, & R. Schwartz (Eds.), *Handbook of family therapy training and supervision.* New York: Guilford.

Faloon, I. R. H. (1991). Behavioral family therapy. In A. S. Gurman & D. P. Kniskern (Eds.) *Handbook of family therapy,* Vol. II (pp. 65–94). New York: Brunner/Mazel.

Ferreira, A. (1953). Family myths and homeostasis. *Archives of General Psychiatry, 9,* 457–463.

Fisch, R. Weakland, J. & Segal, L. (1982). *The tactics of change: Doing therapy briefly.* San Francisco: Jossey-Bass.

Folberg, J. & Milne, A. (1988). *Divorce mediation.* New York: Guilford Press

Framo, J. (1982). *Explorations in marital and family therapy. Selected papers of James L. Framo.* New York: Springer.

Framo, J. (1992). *Family-of-origin therapy: An intergenerational approach.* New York: Brunner/Mazel.

Freedman, J., & Combs, G. (1996). *Narrative therapy: The social construction of preferred realities.* New York: W. W. Norton.

Goldenberg, I., & Goldenberg, H. (1996). *Family therapy: An overview.* 4th ed. Pacific Grove, CA: Brooks/Cole.

Greenberg, G. S. (1977). The family interactional perspective: A study and examination of the work of Don D. Jackson. *Family Process, 16,* 385–410.

Guerin, P. J. (1971). A family affair. *Georgetown Family* Symposium, Vol. 1. Washington, DC.

Guerin, P. (Ed.) (1976). *Family therapy: Theory and practice.* New York: Gardner Press.

Haley, J. (1963). *Strategies of psychotherapy.* New York: Grune & Stratton.

Haley, J. (1976). Problems of training therapists. In J. Haley (Ed.), *Problem-solving Therapy.* San Francisco: Jossey-Bass.

Haynes, J.M., (1981). *Divorce mediation.* New York: Springer.

Held, B. S. (1990). What's in a name? Some confusions and concerns about constructivism. *Journal of Marital and Family Therapy, 16,* 179–186.

Hoffman, L. (1973). Deviation-amplifying processes in natural groups. In J. Haley (Ed.), *Changing families.* New York: Grune & Stratton.

Hoffman, L. (1981). *Foundations of family therapy.* New York: Basic Books.

Hoffman, L. (1990). Constructing realities: An art of lenses. *Family Process, 29* (1), 1–12.

Hoffman, L. (1992). A reflexive stance for family therapy. In S. McNamee and K. J. Gergen (Eds.), *Therapy as social construction* (pp. 7–24). Newbury Park, CA: Sage.

Holtzworth-Munroe, A. (1991). Behavioral marital therapy. Behavioral family therapy. In A. S. Gurman & D. P. Kniskern (Eds.), *Handbook of family therapy*, Vol. II (pp. 96–133). New York: Brunner/Mazel.

Hoopes, M. & Harper, J. (1987). Birth order roles and sibling positions. In *Individual, marital, & family therapy.* Rockville, MD: Aspen Publishers.

Hughes, R.J., & Kirby, J.J. (2000). Strengthening evaluation strategies for divorcing family support services: Perspective of parent educators, mediators, attorneys and judges. *Family Relations, 49,* 53–62.

Imber-Black, E., (1988). *Families and larger systems: A family therapist's guide through the labyrinth.* New York: Guilford.

Imber-Black, E., Roberts, J., & Whiting, R. (1988). *Rituals in families and family therapy.* New York: W.W. Norton.

Jackson, D. (1965). Family rules: Marital quid pro quo. *Archives of General Psychiatry, 12,* 589–594.

Jacobson, N. S., & Margolin, G. (1979). *Marital therapy: Strategies based on social learning and behavior exchange principles.* New York: Brunner/Mazel.

Jacobson, N. S. & Holtzworth-Munroe, A. (1986). Marital therapy: A social learning–cognitive perspective. In N.S. Jacobson & A.S. Gurman (Eds.), *Clinical handbook of marital therapy.* New York: Guilford.

Jones, J. E. (1994). Chronic anxiety, the adrenocortical response, and differentiation. *Family Systems, 4,* 165–172.

Kaslow, F. (1995). The dynamics of divorce therapy. In R. H. Mikesell, D. D. Lusterman, & S. H. McDaniel (Eds.), *Integrating family therapy: Handbook of family psychology and systems theory* (pp. 272–283). Washington, DC: American Psychological Association.

Kaslow, F. (1981). Divorce and divorce therapy. In A.S. Gurman & D. Kniskern (Eds.), *Handbook of family therapy,* Vol. I (pp. 662–696). New York: Brunner/Mazel.

Kaslow, N., Kaslow, F., & Farber, E. (1999). Theories and techniques of marital and family therapy. In M. Sussman, S. Steinmetz, & G. Peterson, (Eds.), *Handbook of marriage and the family* (pp. 784). New York: Plenum Press.

Keeney, B. P. (1983). *Aesthetics of change.* New York: Guilford Press.

Keeney, B. P., & Sprenkle, D. H. (1982). Ecosystemic epistemology: Critical implications for the aesthetics and pragmatics of family therapy. *Family Process, 21,* 1–19.

Kerr, M. & Bowen, M. (1988). *Family Evaluation.* New York: W. W. Norton.

Laqueur, P. (1973). Multiple family therapy: Questions and answers. In D. Bloch (Ed.), *Techniques of family psychotherapy.* New York: Grune & Stratton.

Liddle, H. (1991). Training and supervision in family therapy: A comprehensive and critical analysis. In A. Gurman & D. Kniskern (Eds.), *Handbook of family therapy, Vol. II* (pp. 638–697). New York: Brunner/Mazel.

MacGregor, R., McDonald, C., & Goolishian, H. A. (1964). *Multiple impact therapy with families.* Hightstown, NY: McGraw-Hill.

Madanes, C. (1981). *Strategic family therapy.* San Francisco: Jossey-Bass.

Madanes, C. (1984). *Behind the one-way mirror: Advances in the practice of strategic therapy.* San Francisco: Jossey-Bass.

Marlow, L., & Sauber. S.R. (1990). *The handbook of divorce mediation.* New York: Plenum Press.

Martin, P.A. (1976). *A marital therapy manual.* NY: Brunner/Mazel.

Maturana, H. R. (1978). Biology of language: The epistemology of reality. In G. A. Miller & E. Lenneberg (Eds.), *Psychology and biology of language and thought.* New York: Academic Press.

McDaniel, S. H., Hepworth, J., &

Doherty, W. J. (1992). *Medical family therapy: A biopsychosocial approach to families with health problems.* New York: Basic Books.

McGoldrick, M., Pearce, J., & Giordano, J. (Eds.) (1982). *Ethnicity in family therapy.* New York: Guilford Press.

McGoldrick, M., & Gerson, R. (1985). *Genograms in family assessment.* New York: W. W. Norton.

McGoldrick, M., Preto, N., Hines, P., & Lee, E. (1991). Ethnicity and family therapy. In A. Gurman & D. Kniskern (Eds.), *Handbook of family therapy,* Vol. II. New York: Bunner/Mazel.

McGoldrick, M., Gerson, R., & Shellenberger, S. (1999). *Genograms: Assessment and intervention* New York: W. W. Norton

Minuchin, S. (1974). *Families and family therapy.* Cambridge: Harvard University Press.

Minuchin, S., & Fishman, H. C. (1981). *Family therapy techniques.* Cambridge, MA: Harvard University Press.

Montalvo, B. (1973). Aspects of live supervision. *Family Process, 12,* 343–359.

Napier, A. Y., & Whitaker, C. A. (1978). *The family crucible.* New York: Harper & Row.

Nichols, M. (1984). *Family therapy: Concepts and methods.* New York: Gardner Press.

Nichols, M. P., & Schwartz, R. C. (1998). *Family therapy: Concepts and methods.* Needham Heights, MA: Allyn & Bacon.

Nichols, W. C., & Everett, C. A. (1986). *Systemic family therapy: An integra-*

tive approach. New York: Guilford Press.

Oberndorf, C. P. (1934). Folie à deux. *International Journal of Psychoanalysis, 15,* 14–24.

O'Hanlon, W. H., & Weiner-Davis, M. (1989). *In search of solutions: A new direction in psychotherapy.* New York: W. W. Norton.

Olson, D. H. (1993). Circumplex model of marital and family systems: Assessing family functioning. In F. Walsh (Ed.), *Normal family processes.* New York: Guilford.

Palazzoli, M., Boscolo, L., Cecchin, G., & Prata, G. (1978). *Paradox and counterparadox.* New York: Jason Aronson.

Palazolli, M., Boscolo, L., Cecchin, G., & Prata, G. (1980). Hypothesizing–circularity–neutrality: Three guidelines for the conductor of the session. *Family Process, 19,* 3–12.

Papp, P. (1980). The Greek chorus and other techniques of family therapy. *Family Process, 19,* 45–57.

Papp, P., Silverstein, O., & Carter, E. (1973). Family sculpting in preventive work with well families. *Family Process, 12,* 197–212.

Patterson, G. R., Reid, J. B., Jones, R. R. & Conger, R. E. (1975). *A social learning approach to family intervention.* Eugene, Oregon: Castalia.

Pincus, L. & Dare, C. (1978). *Secrets in the family.* New York: Pantheon.

Sager, C. (1976). *Marriage contracts and couples therapy.* New York: Brunner/Mazel.

Sager, C. (1981). Couples therapy and marriage contracts. In A. Gurman & D. Kniskern (Eds.), *Handbook of family therapy,* Vol. 1 (pp. 85–130) New York: Brunner/Mazel.

Satir, V. (1967). *Conjoint family therapy.* Palo Alto, CA: Science and Behavior Books.

Scharff, J. S. & Scharff, D. (1987). *Object relations family therapy.* Northvale, NJ: Jason Aronson.

Schnarch, D. (1991). *Constructing the sexual crucible: An integration of sexual and marital therapy.* New York: W. W. Norton.

Schwartz, R., Liddle, H., & Breunlin, D. (1988). Muddles in live supervision. In H.A. Liddle, D.C. Breunlin, & R.C. Schwartz (Eds.), *Handbook of family therapy training and supervision.* New York: Guilford Press.

Seaburn, D., Landau-Stanton, J., & Horwitz, S. (1995). Core techniques in family therapy. In R.H. Mikesell, D.D. Lusterman, & S.H. McDaniel (Eds.), *Integrating family therapy: Handbook of family psychology and systems theory* (pp. 5–26). Washington, DC: APA.

Seaburn, D., Lorenz, A. D., Gunn, W. B., Gawinski, B. A., & Mauksch, L. B. (1996). *Models of collaboration: A guide for mental health professionals working with health care practitioners.* New York: Basic Books.

Segal, L. (1991). Brief therapy: The MRI approach. In A. S. Gurman & D. P. Kniskern (Eds.), *Handbook of family therapy,* Vol. II (pp. 171–199). New York: Brunner/Mazel.

Skynner, A. (1976). *Systems of family and marital therapy.* New York: Brunner/Mazel.

Skynner, A. (1981). *An open-systems, group-analytic approach to family therapy.* New York: Brunner/Mazel.

Speck, R. & Attneave, C. (1973). *Family networks*. New York: Pantheon.

Sprenkle, D., & Storm, C. (1983). Divorce therapy outcome research: A substantive and methodological review. *Journal of Marital and Family Therapy, 9*, 239–258.

Steinglass, P. (1978). The conceptualization of marriage from a systems theory perspective. In T. J. Paolino & B. S. McCrady (Eds.), *Marriage and marital therapy* (pp. 361–402). New York: Brunner/Mazel.

Stierlin, H. (1974). *Separating parents and adolescents*. New York: Quadrangle.

Toman, W. (1976). *Family constellation*. New York: Springer.

Tomm, K. (1984). One perspective on the Milan systematic approach: Part I. Overview of the development, theory and practice. *Journal of Marital and Family Therapy, 10*, 113–125.

Tomm, K. (1987). Interventive interviewing: Part II. Reflexive questioning as a means to enable self-healing. *Family Process, 26*, 167–183.

Tomm, K. (1988). Interventive interviewing: Part III. Intending to ask linear, circular, strategic, or reflexive questions. *Family Process, 27*, 1–15.

Vogel, E. & Bell, N. W. (1960). The emotionally disturbed child as a family scapegoat. In N. W. Bell & E. Vogel (Eds.), *The family* (pp. 382–397). Glencoe, IL: Free Press.

Von Bertalanffy, L. (1968). *General systems theory*. New York: Braziller.

Von Bertalanffy, L. (1974). General systems theory and psychiatry. In S. Arieti (Ed.), *American handbook of psychiatry*, Vol.1 (2nd Ed.). New York: Basic Books.

Walters, M., Carter, B., Papp, P., & Silverstein, O. (1988). *The invisible web: Gender patterns in family relationships*. New York: Guilford.

Watzlawick, P. (1984). *The invented reality*. New York: W. W. Norton.

Watzlawick, P. (1988). *Ultra-solutions: How to fail most successfully*. New York: W. W. Norton.

Watzlawick, P., Beavin, J., & Jackson, D. (1967). *Pragmatics of human communication*. New York: W. W. Norton.

Watzlawick, P., Weakland, J., & Fisch, R. (1974). *Change: Principles of problem formation and problem resolution*. New York: W. W. Norton.

Watzlawick, P., & Weakland, J. (Eds.) (1977). *The interactional view: Studies at the Mental Research Institute 1965-1974*. New York: W. W. Norton.

Weber, T., & Levine, F. (1995). Engaging the family: An integrative approach. In R.H. Mikesell, D.D. Lusterman, & S.H. McDaniel (Eds.), *Integrating family therapy: Handbook of family psychology and systems theory* (pp. 45–72). Washington, DC: APA.

Weeks, G. R., & Treat, S. (1992). *Couples in treatment: Techniques and approaches for effective practice*. New York: Brunner/Mazel.

Whitaker, C. (1982). *From psyche to system: The evolving theory of Carl Whitaker*. J. Neil & D. Kniskern (Eds.). New York: Guilford.

Whitaker, C. (1989). *Midnight musings*

of a family therapist. New York: W. W. Norton.

Whitaker, C. & Bumberry, W. A. (1988). *Dancing with the family: A symbolic–experiential approach.* New York: Brunner/Mazel.

Whitchurch, B., & Constantine, L. (1993). Systems theory. In P. Boss, W. Doherty, R. LaRossa, W. Schumm, & S. Steinmetz (Eds.), *Sourcebook of family theories and methods: A contextual approach* (pp. 325–355). New York: Plenum.

White, M. (1992). Deconstruction and therapy. In D. Epston & M. White, *Experience, contradiction, narrative, & imagination: Selected papers of David Epstone & Michael White 1989–1991* (pp. 109–152). Adelaide, South Australia: Dulwich Centre Publications.

White, M. (1997). *Narratives of therapists' lives.* Adelaide, South Australia: Dulwich Centre Publications.

White, M., & Epston, D. (1990). *Narrative means to therapeutic ends.* New York: W. W. Norton.

Winch, R. (1954). The theory of complementary need in mate selection: An analytic and descriptive study. *American Sociological Review, 19,* 241–249.

Wynne, L. (1961). The study of intrafamilial alignments and splits in exploratory family therapy. In N. Ackerman, F. Beatman, & S. Sherman (Eds.), *Exploring the base for family therapy.* New York: Family Service Association.

Wynne, L. (1988). *The state of the art in family therapy.* New York: Family Process.

Wynne, L., Ryckoff, I., Day, J., & Hirsch, S. (1958). Pseudomutuality in family relations of schizophrenics. *Psychiatry, 21,* 205–220.

Wynne, L., McDaniel, S., & Weber, T. (1987). *Systems consultation.* New York: Guilford.

Zinner, J., & Shapiro, R. L. (1989). Projective identification as a mode of perception and behavior in families of adolescents. In J. S. Scharff (Ed.), *Foundations of objection relations family therapy.* Northvale, NJ: Jason Aronson.

Zuk, G. (1971). *Family therapy: A triadic-based approach.* New York: Human Sciences Press.

Notes

Notes